IT'S GREAT TO BE A FAN IN FLORIDA

by Matthew McCabe

FOCUS READERS

FOCUS READERS

www.focusreaders.com

Focus Readers is distributed by North Star Editions:
sales@northstareditions.com | 888-417-0195

Produced for Focus Readers by Red Line Editorial.

Photographs ©: Mark LoMoglio/Icon Sportswire/AP Images, cover (top), 1 (top); Wilfredo Lee/AP Images, cover (bottom left), 1 (bottom left); Del Mecum/Cal Sport Media/AP Images, cover (bottom right), 1 (bottom right); Felix Mizioznikov/Shutterstock Images, 4–5; pisaphotography/Shutterstock Images, 7; Sean Pavone/Shutterstock Images, 9; Red Line Editorial, 11, 21, 29; Lynne Sladky/AP Images, 12–13, 38–39; Paul Spinelli/AP Images, 15; Ryan Remiorz/AP Images, 17; Nick Wass/AP Images, 19; Bill Ingraham/AP Images, 23; Bill Ragan/Shutterstock Images, 24–25; Doug Murray/Icon Sportswire/AP Images, 27; Steve Nesius/AP Images, 31; Jimmy Rash/Cal Sport Media/AP Images, 32–33; f11photo/Shutterstock Images, 35; Pete Hoffman/Shutterstock Images, 37; AP Images, 41; Action Sports Photography/Shutterstock Images, 43; photogolfer/Shutterstock Images, 45

ISBN
978-1-63517-928-6 (hardcover)
978-1-64185-030-8 (paperback)
978-1-64185-232-6 (ebook pdf)
978-1-64185-131-2 (hosted ebook)

Library of Congress Control Number: 2018931994

Printed in the United States of America
Mankato, MN
May, 2018

ABOUT THE AUTHOR

Matthew McCabe has been a freelance writer since 2008. What began as a hobby turned into a career. In addition to writing numerous other titles within series such as Change Makers, he is also a contract marketing and advertising copywriter. He lives in Plymouth, Minnesota, with his wife and two children.

TABLE OF CONTENTS

CLEVELAN
CLEVELANDER.COM

CHAPTER 1

THE SUNSHINE STATE

For good reason, Florida is called the "Sunshine State." The warm weather and sunny days have attracted people to the area for thousands of years. With the ability to be outdoors year-round, it's no wonder Florida is a sports destination. Florida has its own teams to be proud of, but it also attracts visiting fans from around the country in every sport.

Palm trees are everywhere in the Sunshine State, even outside the home of the Miami Marlins.

Florida's **climate** first drew people to the area more than 10,000 years ago. People known as Paleoindians arrived searching for mineral water sources. The first American Indian settlements were near wetlands. By the year 700 CE, **tribes** such as the Timucua and Apalachee began to form. For the next 700 years, these tribes were the only people to live in the area.

European explorers saw the Florida coastline for the first time in 1498. A few years later, in 1513, Spanish explorer Juan Ponce de León became the first European to go ashore. He named the area *La Florida*, meaning "land of flowers." Approximately 300,000 American Indians lived in the Florida region at the time of Ponce de León's arrival. However, within 80 years, slavery and disease resulted in death for most American Indians.

The Ponce de León Inlet Light is one of the tallest lighthouses in the United States.

Members of the Calusa tribe killed Ponce de León in 1521 when he tried to establish a **colony** on their land. Other Spanish explorers tried to establish colonies in Florida, but all failed until 1565. That was the year Pedro Menéndez founded the city of St. Augustine. It was one of the first permanent European settlements in North America.

From the 1600s to the mid-1800s, various powers fought over Florida. The Spanish and French both had towns or forts in Florida. The British invaded several times.

Members of other native tribes came to Florida in the 1700s to escape wars farther to the north. Some of these tribes merged to become the Seminoles. From 1817 to 1858, there were three wars between the Seminoles and the US Army. Known as the Seminole Wars, all three conflicts started because of invasions by the US Army. Between the second and third wars, more US citizens moved to Florida. With the increased population of white settlers, Florida joined the United States as a new state in 1845. After the third Seminole War ended in 1858, only 200 Seminoles were still alive. They struggled to rebuild their society.

Established in 1565, St. Augustine is one of the oldest cities in the United States.

Natural resources were one of the major reasons new people moved to Florida. Large amounts of land were available for farming. Sugarcane, fruit, and lumber were major exports. And the state's long coastline offered ports for shipping and naval activity.

The modern Florida **economy** is built on many of the same things, including **agriculture**. The state's mild climate makes it great for farming.

Florida is still famous today for its oranges. Mild temperatures also attract plenty of tourists. The warm weather and sandy beaches drew 113 million visitors to Florida in 2016.

Florida is now the fourth-largest US state by population, with more than 19 million residents. Most Floridians live along the coasts. Florida has coastline on the Gulf of Mexico and Atlantic Ocean. Many people live in the big cities that started out as ports. Miami, Tampa, Orlando, and Jacksonville are the largest cities. Orlando is the only large city not on the coast.

THINK ABOUT IT

Florida has a warm, humid climate. It has been inhabited for thousands of years. How do you think early inhabitants lived without air conditioning in Florida?

All those cities host major pro sports teams. Some also have college sports, motorsports, and individual sports such as golf. When it comes to sports and recreation, Florida seems to have it all.

FLORIDA'S BIGGEST CITIES

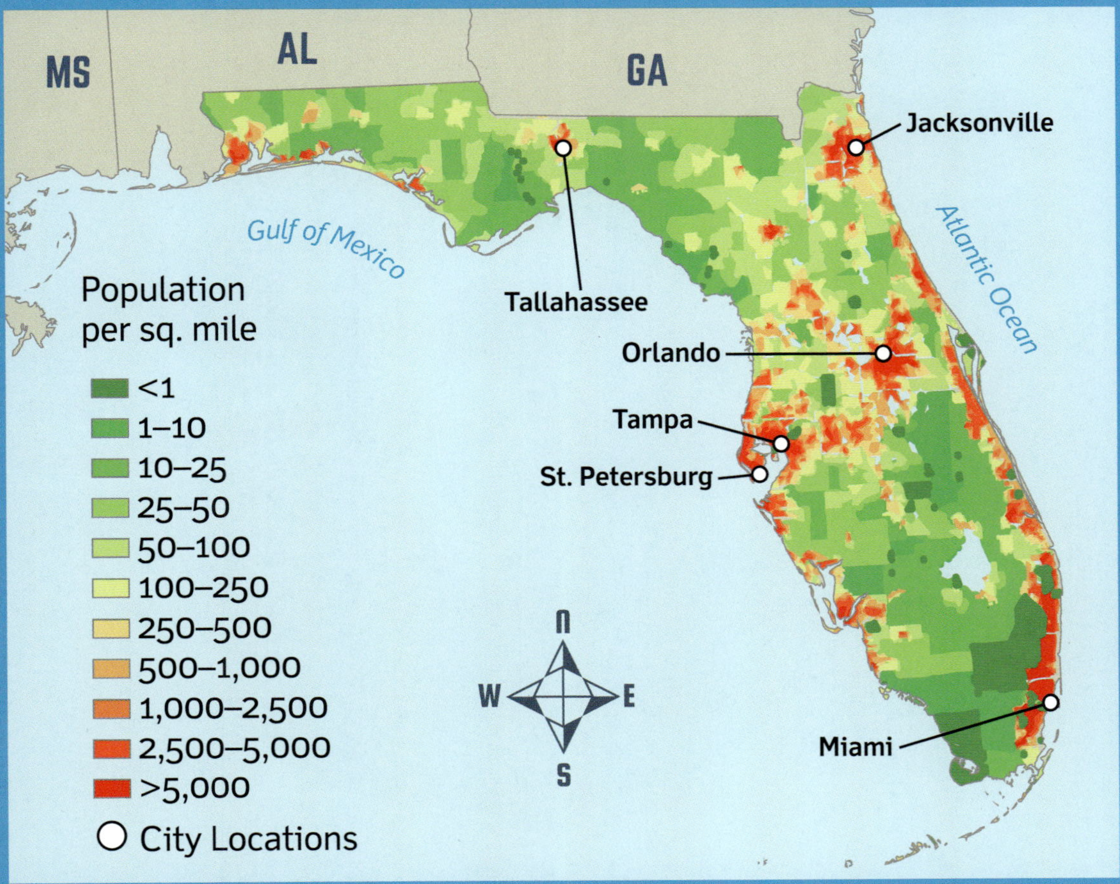

CHAPTER 2

PRO SPORTS IN FLORIDA

The weather in Florida makes outdoor sports easy to enjoy all year round. But the state does not limit itself to just outdoor sports. People in Florida enjoy indoor sports as well, including ice hockey. The state is home to 11 professional sports franchises. Each major professional North American league has at least one team in Florida.

The Miami Dolphins of the National Football League (NFL) are the oldest pro team in Florida.

Quarterback Dan Marino played his entire hall-of-fame career with the Miami Dolphins.

They are also the most successful. Founded in 1966, the Dolphins won back-to-back Super Bowls in 1972 and 1973. The 1972 Dolphins are the only undefeated team in the Super Bowl era. They won every game, including the playoffs, to finish the season with a record of 17–0. The Dolphins have also been to three other Super Bowls and won 13 division titles as of 2017.

The Tampa Bay Buccaneers were the second NFL team in Florida. They were founded in 1976. Known as the Bucs, they were one of the worst teams in the NFL when they started out. In fact, they lost the first 26 games in team history. But they have made major improvements since then. The Bucs won their first Super Bowl in 2003.

Florida's third NFL team is the Jacksonville Jaguars. The Jaguars are one of the newest NFL teams, but they made it to the conference

Jon Gruden coached the Bucs to a Super Bowl championship after the 2002 season.

championship after the 1996, 1999, and 2017 seasons. The Jaguars are Jacksonville's only major pro team. The metro area has a population of less than two million, making it one of the smallest markets in the NFL.

The Dolphins were the only pro team in Miami until 1988. That's when the Miami Heat joined the National Basketball Association (NBA) as one of four **expansion teams**. The Heat struggled at first but became an Eastern Conference powerhouse by the mid-1990s. The Heat won NBA titles in 2006, 2012, and 2013.

The Orlando Magic followed the Heat into the NBA in 1989. The team has had some great players, such as Shaquille O'Neal and Dwight Howard, but has yet to win an NBA title. The Magic played in the NBA Finals in 1995 and 2009 but won just a single game combined.

Ice hockey came to the Sunshine State in 1992. The Tampa Bay Lightning joined the National Hockey League (NHL) that season. After some early struggles, the team broke through in 2004 to win the state's first Stanley Cup. The Lightning

The Lightning became the southernmost NHL team to win the Stanley Cup in 2004.

also appeared in the 2015 Final but could not win a second Cup.

The Florida Panthers joined the NHL in 1993. The Panthers are the southernmost franchise in the league. They are located in Sunrise, just outside of Miami. The Panthers made it to the Stanley Cup Final in just their third NHL season.

But they lost to the Colorado Avalanche in a four-game sweep.

Florida has long been a destination for Major League Baseball (MLB) **spring training**. The state has also been home to many minor league teams over the years. But Florida had no MLB team of its own until 1993. The Florida Marlins joined MLB that season as an expansion team. The team made its first-ever playoff appearance in 1997 as a wild-card team. Surprisingly, they won the World Series. The Marlins added another World Series title in 2003. They changed their name to the Miami Marlins in 2011, just before they opened a new ballpark near downtown Miami.

Baseball came to the Tampa Bay area in 1998. Originally known as the Tampa Bay Devil Rays, the team was one of the worst in baseball for its first 10 seasons. In 2008, the team shortened

Slugger Miguel Cabrera is the Marlins' all-time leader in batting average.

its name to the Rays. That was also the year the team made its first playoff appearance. The Rays reached the World Series but lost to the Philadelphia Phillies in five games.

Florida's newest teams play in Orlando. The city now has two major professional soccer teams.

Orlando City Soccer Club joined Major League Soccer (MLS) in 2015. The Orlando Pride play in the National Women's Soccer League (NWSL). In 2017, the Pride made its first playoff appearance but lost to Portland Thorns FC.

Florida's teams reflect the state's unique environment through their names. The wetlands, reefs, and bays of Florida host a wide variety of natural wildlife. Marlins, stingrays, dolphins, panthers, and more all call Florida home. These animals all inspired Florida team names.

The weather in Florida is usually great, but there are occasional storms, rain, and even hurricanes. And in the summer, the heat can be intense. For these reasons, the Marlins opened a retractable-roof stadium in 2012. That means fans can enjoy the sunshine when the weather is nice, and they can stay protected from the elements when the weather doesn't cooperate. And in Tampa, the Rays play indoors under the dome and in the air conditioning of Tropicana Field.

MAP OF FLORIDA'S TEAMS

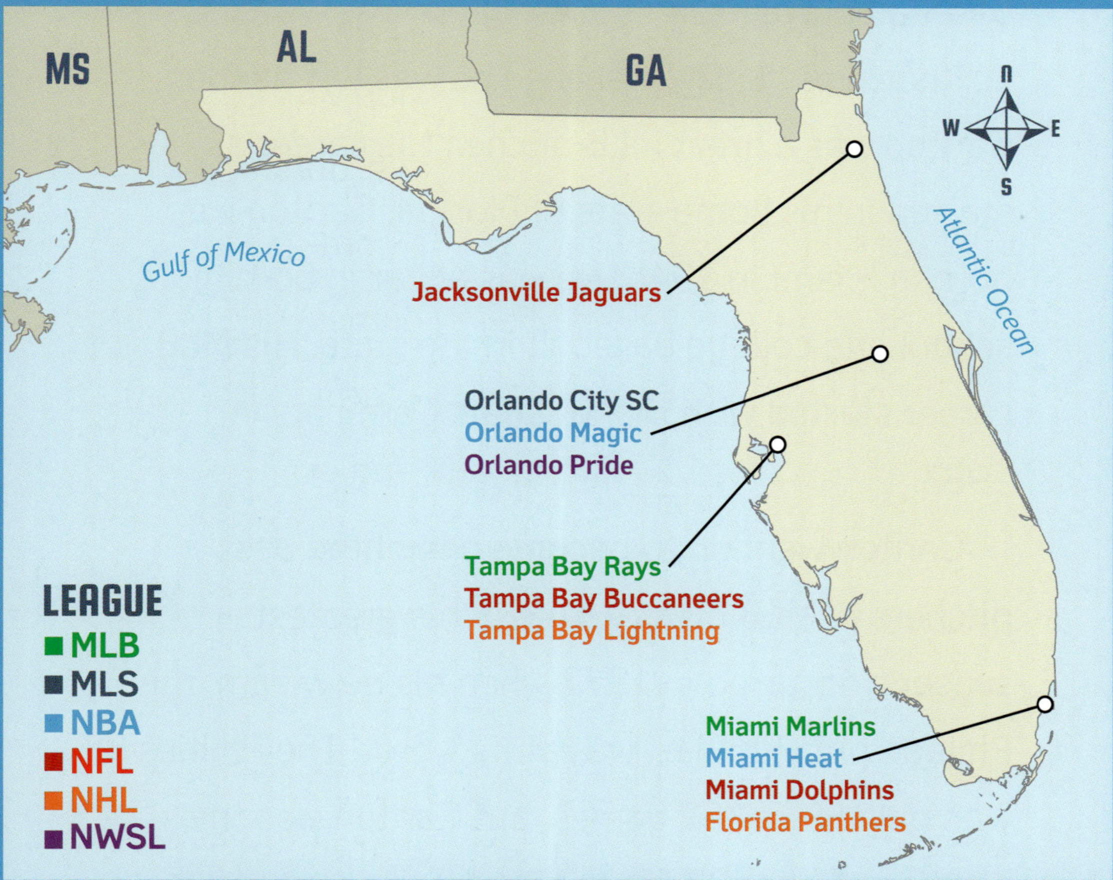

STEVE CARLTON

Steve Carlton's baseball career ended before Major League Baseball came to Florida. Carlton retired in 1988, five years before the Marlins were founded. However, Carlton is Florida's greatest baseball player.

Known as "Lefty" because he was left handed, Carlton was a great MLB pitcher. His career started in his home state of Florida. Carlton was born in Miami in 1944. He was a star in both high school and college baseball in the state. His MLB career started with the St. Louis Cardinals in 1963.

Carlton went on to become one of the best pitchers in MLB history. One of his greatest seasons occurred in 1972 when his new team, the Philadelphia Phillies, was at its worst. The Phillies won only 59 of 162 games, but Carlton was the winning pitcher 27 times that season.

Steve Carlton threw 30 complete games in 1972, more than the entire National League did in 2017.

Over his career, Carlton won 329 games. That is the second-most among left-handed pitchers. He was the first pitcher to win four Cy Young Awards. Carlton was elected to the Baseball Hall of Fame in 1994.

BEN HILL GRIFFIN STADIUM
Publix
SUNTRUST
WELCOME TO THE SWAMP
GATOR COUNTRY

CHAPTER 3

MAJOR COLLEGE RIVALRIES

From high school to the NFL, Floridians love football. The state has been extremely successful on the **gridiron**, especially at the college level. These schools have long histories, unique traditions, and passionate fans. Florida has seven major **Division I** football programs.

The University of Florida, Florida State University, and the University of Miami compete in some of college football's toughest conferences.

Ben Hill Griffin Stadium, home of the University of Florida Gators, is the largest stadium in Florida.

The University of Florida is in the Southeastern Conference, while Florida State and Miami play in the Atlantic Coast Conference.

The University of Florida Gators started in Gainesville in 1906. It seems hard to believe now, but it took nearly a century for the Gators to win a national championship. Former Gators player Steve Spurrier became head coach in 1990. He led the Gators to their first title in 1996. Florida won two more national championships in 2006 and 2008 with Urban Meyer as head coach. The Gators' home stadium is nicknamed "the Swamp." Spurrier came up with the nickname in 1992 because a swamp is a place where alligators are king.

Down south, the University of Miami started playing football in 1926. Known as the Miami Hurricanes, the program was at its most dominant

Mascot Sebastian the Ibis leads the Miami Hurricanes onto the field.

in the 1980s. Miami won its first three national championships in 1983, 1987, and 1989. The Hurricanes won additional titles in 1991 and 2001.

Up in the panhandle of Florida, Florida State briefly had a football program from 1902 to 1904. But it did not have football again until 1947.

Although Florida State started much later, the Seminoles have enjoyed near-equal success to their rivals. The Seminoles won national titles in 1993 and 1999 under legendary head coach Bobby Bowden.

These major college football teams have serious **rivalries** with one another. Miami and Florida State were the premier programs in the 1980s and 1990s. The Hurricanes and Seminoles combined for six national titles over the two decades. Florida and Florida State have their own rivalry. The two teams first met in 1958, and they have played every year since.

Not all of Florida's Division I schools play in big conferences. Florida Atlantic University, Florida International University, the University of Central Florida, and the University of South Florida play in smaller conferences. But that doesn't mean these schools don't have great teams. In 2017, for example, Central Florida had the only undefeated season in the country by a Division I team. They even got a parade at Walt Disney World.

FLORIDA'S DIVISION I FOOTBALL TEAMS

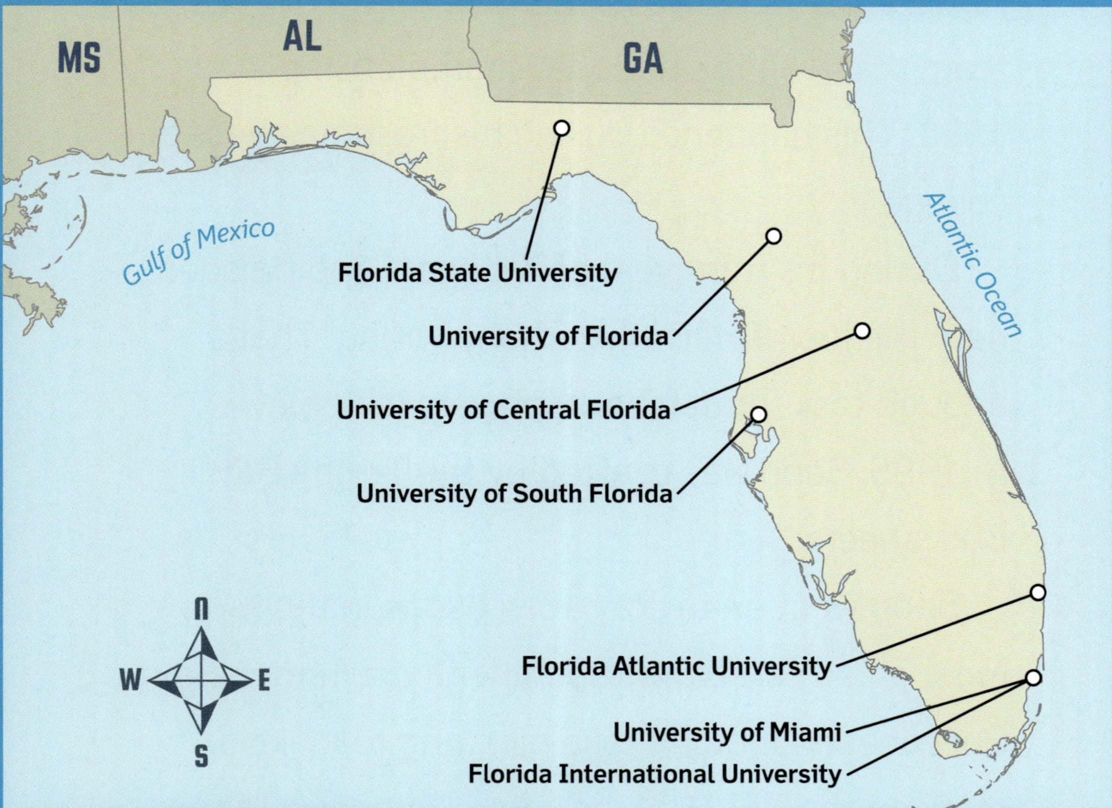

WARREN SAPP

Warren Sapp is one of the few Florida athletes to have played at all levels in his home state. Sapp was born near Orlando, Florida, in 1972. He played high school football in the area as a kid. He went on to play college football for the Miami Hurricanes. Sapp was a member of the Hurricanes team that won the national championship in 1991. This happened during his freshman year of college.

During his third year of college, Sapp finished near the top of Heisman Trophy voting. That's a tough task for defensive players to achieve. In 1995, Sapp was **drafted** by the Tampa Bay Buccaneers.

Sapp went on to play 13 seasons in the NFL. Most of his career was spent with the Tampa Bay Buccaneers. It didn't take him long to make a mark on the NFL. He was voted Defensive Player

Warren Sapp had his jersey No. 99 retired by the Bucs in 2013.

of the Year in 1999. He helped the team win its first division title in 18 seasons.

In 2002, Sapp led the team to a Super Bowl victory. It was Tampa's first Super Bowl. Sapp left Tampa after the 2003 season and ended his career with the Oakland Raiders. He was elected to the Pro Football Hall of Fame in 2013.

GATORS
37

CHAPTER 4

ENDLESS SUMMER, ENDLESS BASEBALL

Baseball players are sometimes known as the Boys of Summer. Baseball leagues across the United States play during the summer to take advantage of the warmest weather. Since Florida's climate is warm all year round, the state naturally became a haven for baseball.

December and January have the lowest average temperature each year in Florida. But that's still a relatively warm 61 degrees Fahrenheit (16°C).

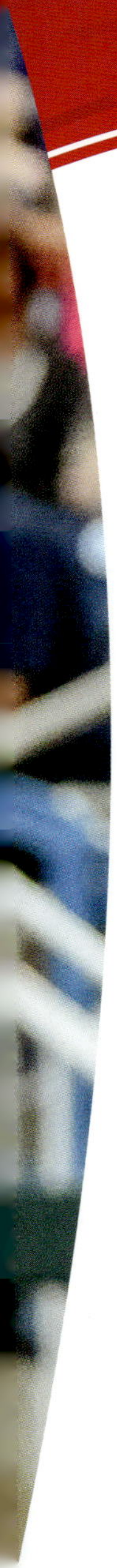

From T-ball to college, Florida is a great place to grow up playing baseball.

The highest average temperature comes in July and August, when it shoots up to 82 degrees Fahrenheit (28°C). While Florida gets a lot of sun, it is not the sunniest place in the country. That honor goes to Arizona. But Florida is not far behind, and some areas are sunnier than others. The sunniest place in the state is Key West, which sees sun for 76 percent of its daylight hours.

With so much warmth and sunshine, Florida is ideal for baseball. And that means the kids who grow up in the state have an advantage over their cold-weather counterparts. In the 2017 MLB season, for example, Florida-born players were the second-largest group in MLB, behind only California-born players. Some of these players were among the best in baseball, such as Chicago Cubs first baseman Anthony Rizzo and Boston Red Sox ace Chris Sale.

Key West is the sunniest place in Florida and the southernmost point in the US mainland.

Florida and California are closely matched when it comes to baseball. California creates more college baseball talent. But Florida creates far more high school baseball athletes. Numerous MLB athletes played high school baseball in Florida. All-Star slugger Alex Rodriguez grew up in Miami and played high school baseball there.

More recently, National League Most Valuable Players (MVPs) Ryan Braun (University of Miami) and Buster Posey (Florida State) played college baseball in Florida.

Two of Florida's greatest baseball players are Tim Raines and Chipper Jones. Raines was born and raised near Orlando. He played high school baseball for Seminole High School in his hometown of Sanford. Raines was remarkably fast. He led the National League in stolen bases four years in a row starting with his rookie year in 1981. He made seven All-Star Games. Raines was elected to the Hall of Fame in 2017.

THINK ABOUT IT

Florida and Arizona both host spring training. Florida is humid and hot, while Arizona is dry and hot. Which climate do you think is better to play in?

Florida native Chipper Jones hit 468 career home runs in 19 big-league seasons.

Jones was an All-USA selection in 1990, batting .488 for his Jacksonville high school. He was elected to the National Baseball Hall of Fame in 2018, the eighth Florida-born player to have the honor. And with more and more Floridians doing well in MLB, there will almost certainly be more Hall of Famers in the future.

CHAPTER 5

NATIONAL SPORTS DESTINATION

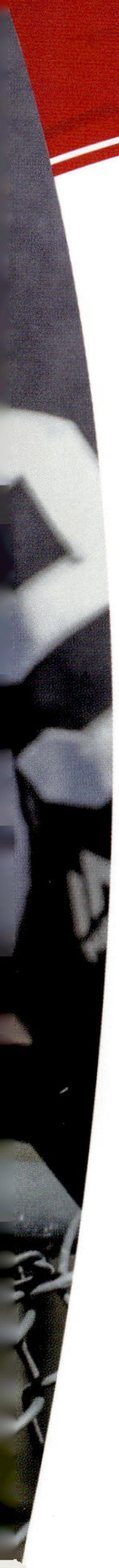

Florida's weather makes it an ideal place for just about any sport. But while Florida's fans get to enjoy great weather all year round, fans from around the country love to experience Florida as well. One of the biggest draws for fans is MLB spring training.

Spring training for MLB teams begins in February, and 15 teams call Florida home while they prepare for the start of the regular season.

Fans can get up close to their favorite players at spring training in Florida.

The teams play one another in an informal competition known as the Grapefruit League. This name recalls Florida's citrus industry.

The history of spring training actually predates other baseball leagues in Florida. In 2013, Florida marked 125 years of hosting spring training. The first team to train in Florida was the 1888 Washington Nationals (no relation to the current Nationals). This team went to Jacksonville to train for the upcoming season. But apparently they didn't train hard enough, because the team folded a year later.

The Philadelphia Athletics went to Jacksonville for spring training in 1900. This was the first team to spend a full spring in Florida. The state began to earn a reputation as a great place for teams to train. Only six existing MLB teams have never held spring training in Florida.

Babe Ruth (left) and the New York Yankees trained in Florida in the 1920s.

Over the years, more than 30 cities in Florida have hosted spring training. Spring training is a big part of the local economy in those cities. In 2017, more than 1.5 million people visited Florida for baseball. The state has earned $753 million from hosting spring training. These cities also form bonds with their teams. Seven teams have been in the same city for 25 years or more.

The Detroit Tigers began training in Lakeland way back in 1946.

Florida's weather also makes it a big draw for auto racing fans. The Daytona 500 is the premier event in stock car racing. The National Association for Stock Car Auto Racing (NASCAR) holds the race each February. It is known as the Great American Race. Drivers used to race on the beaches of Daytona, but now they compete at the 2.5-mile (4.0-km) Daytona International Speedway. The track can hold more than 100,000 fans.

Farther south, Homestead-Miami Speedway is another major track. Opened in 1995, the track hosts the championship race for NASCAR in November each year. Homestead-Miami is a mile shorter than Daytona, but it still features exciting high-speed action.

NASCAR's top series comes to Daytona for two races a year.

Football bowl games are another major winter draw for out-of-state fans. These games match up the best teams in college football every December and January. Florida hosted eight bowl games in the 2017–18 season. The state has some of the oldest and most prestigious bowl games in the country, such as the Orange Bowl and Citrus Bowl.

When it comes to pro football, no state has hosted the sport's biggest event more than Florida. Miami's hosting of Super Bowl LIV in 2020 marks the 16th time that Florida has hosted the big game. That Super Bowl is the 11th for Miami, which is the most of any city. Jacksonville has hosted one Super Bowl, and Tampa has hosted four.

Golf is a sport that draws people to Florida, both to watch and to play. Florida has some of the most famous and beautiful golf courses in the United States. It also has the most, with more than 1,250 beautifying the state. Palm Beach County has more courses than any other county in the nation. Florida has hosted two of golf's **major tournaments**: the 1971 and 1981 PGA Championships. Many pro golfers live in Florida so they can practice year-round.

The island green on the 17th hole at the TPC at Sawgrass is one of the most famous holes in golf.

Florida's weather may allow it to host a wide variety of sports, but that's not the only reason it's a great sports state. It's also because of the fans' dedication to their teams. Whether it's hometown fans cheering on the Dolphins or faraway fans coming to see their teams in spring training, Florida is the home of championship teams and championship fans.

FOCUS ON

FLORIDA

Write your answers on a separate piece of paper.

1. Write a paragraph summarizing the main ideas of Chapter 1.

2. Which Florida sports team do you think has been the most successful to date? Why?

3. How many college football championships has the University of Miami won?

- **A.** one
- **B.** five
- **C.** seven

4. Why does Florida host so many college football bowl games?

- **A.** because the state pays other teams to travel there
- **B.** because the state has some of the best football teams in the nation
- **C.** because the state's weather is nice even in December and January

Answer key on page 48.

GLOSSARY

agriculture
The science of farming animals or plants.

climate
The average weather conditions of a particular place or region.

colony
An area controlled by a country that is far away.

Division I
The top level of college sports in the United States.

drafted
Chosen by a team when entering a sports league.

economy
A system of goods, services, money, and jobs.

expansion teams
New teams that are added to a league.

gridiron
A name for an American football field.

major tournaments
The biggest annual tournaments in golf: the Masters, the US Open, the British Open, and the PGA Championship.

rivalries
Ongoing and frequent competitions between two players or teams.

spring training
A time when players get ready for the upcoming season.

tribes
Groups of people that share a common heritage.

TO LEARN MORE

BOOKS

Hamilton, John. *Florida: The Sunshine State*. Minneapolis, MN: Abdo Publishing, 2017.

Howell, Brian. *Florida Gators*. Minneapolis, MN: Abdo Publishing, 2014.

Orr, Tamra B. *Florida*. New York: Scholastic, 2018.

NOTE TO EDUCATORS

Visit **www.focusreaders.com** to find lesson plans, activities, links, and other resources related to this title.

INDEX

Answer Key: 1. Answers will vary; **2.** Answers will vary; **3.** B; **4.** C